There are over 60 different types of deer in the world, and they come in many shapes and sizes. Usually, only male deer have antlers on their heads. By the way, the plural of deer is still deer! Outline and colour the deer on this page, and make them skip around.

Deer are eaten by many animals like tigers, lions, wolves...
and even large snakes! As naturally gentle animals, most of them
protect themselves by running away rather than fighting back.
Some deer can run at speeds of up to 70 kilometres an hour!

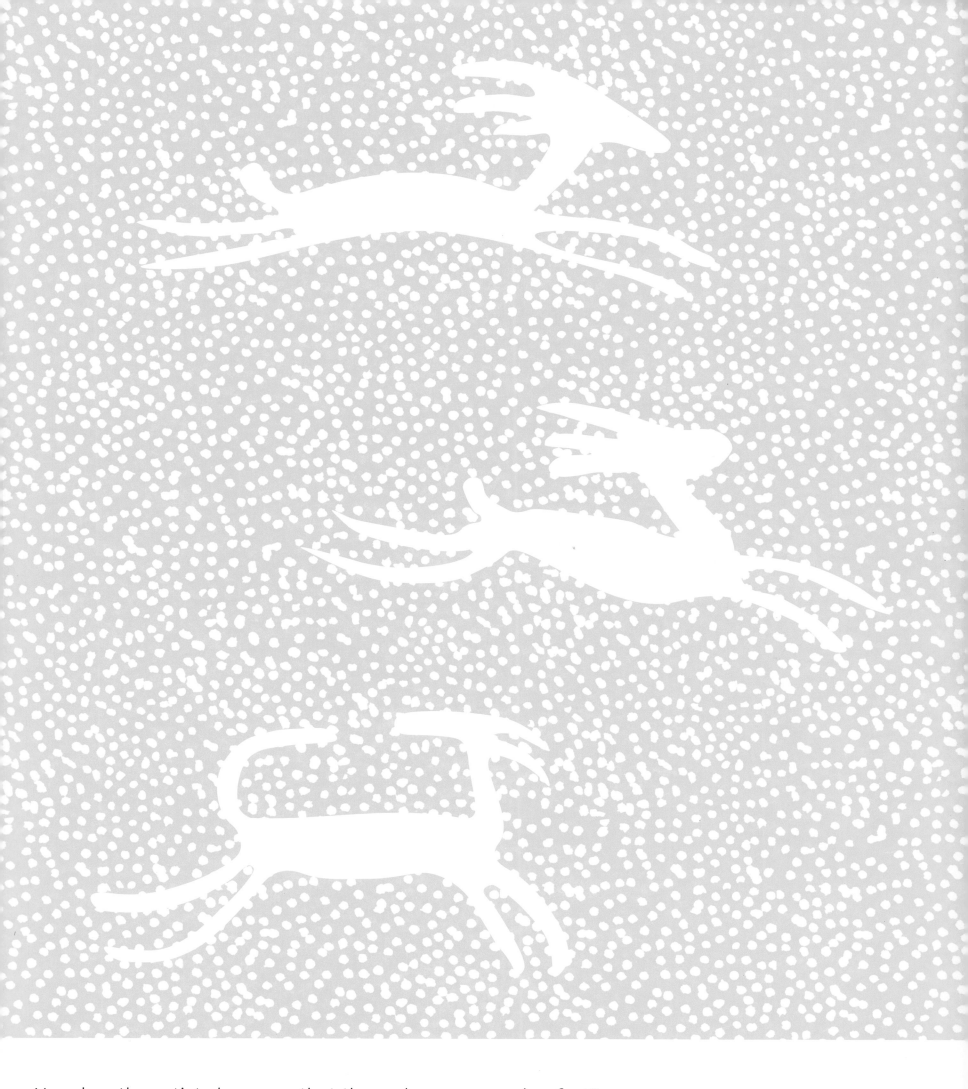

How has the artist shown us that these deer are running fast?
Which one of them is looking back? Colour them all in!

Most deer live in forests or grasslands. Deer are herbivores, which means they eat only plants. They spend a lot of time looking for grass, leaves and fruit to eat. Outline and colour these plants and also draw some more food for the spotted deer to eat. Do you see any other creatures wanting to share her food? Outline and colour them in.

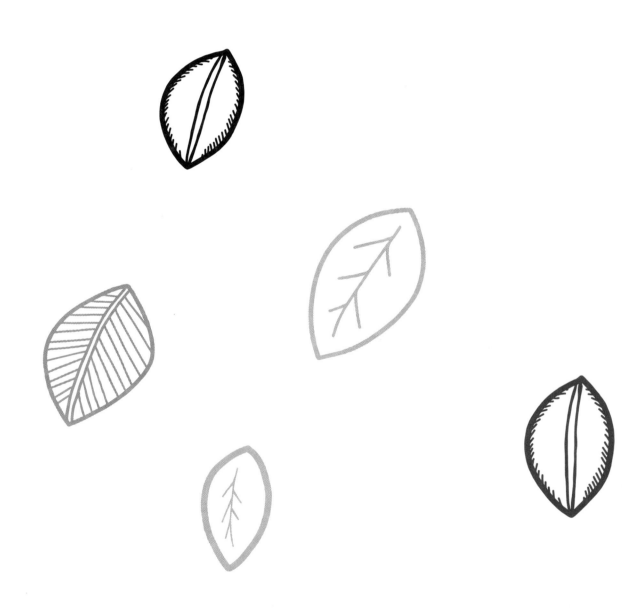

Deer are very curious animals and enjoy exploring their surroundings.
Their senses of smell and sight are very strong. What do you think these
deer could be looking at? Complete the picture.

Deer move about in groups called herds. The artist has given the deer in this herd different patterns, to show the fur that covers their bodies. Their fur is longer in winter, to keep them warm, and shorter in summer, so they stay cool. Draw different patterns on the deer, and give them different coats for summer and winter.

Deer are very beautiful creatures, with large eyes and elegant bodies covered with fur in different patterns. This artist has chosen to decorate her deer with bold patterns. Decorate the deer on the facing page.

This beautiful spotted deer looks really sweet and gentle. But how can
we tell? Because of her eyes? The mouth? Or the way she's sitting?

Make her twin different: draw different eyes and eyebrows, change the shape of her mouth, and give her different fur. What kind of character is she?

Only male deer have antlers, except in the case of reindeer, where both male and female deer grow antlers. The artist has drawn magnificent antlers on this deer, making them look like the branches of a tree. Let your imagination loose, and extend the antlers to fill the page. You can even add leaves to them... to show how a deer is connected to the forest. Give the young deer antlers too!

Even though a herd of deer are similar to each other, maybe you
want to mix them up a bit? Add different kinds of deer to this page,
going back through the book to pick up the ones you like.